The Collected Poetry of
Abraham Lincoln

THE COLLECTED POETRY OF

Abraham Lincoln

Privately Printed · Springfield, Illinois · 1971

Contents

Introduction

Abraham Lincoln was not an assiduous reader. In fact, his law partner and biographer, William H. Herndon, said of him that he read less and thought more than any prominent man of his time. But this statement should not be taken literally. At New Salem, Jack Kelso, a lazy dreamer who preferred hunting and fishing to working, introduced the young Lincoln to Shakespeare and Burns, authors whom he cherished all his life. Midway in his presidency Lincoln wrote to the actor, James H. Hackett: "Some of Shakespeare's plays I have never read; while others I have gone over perhaps as frequently as any unprofessional reader. Among the latter are Lear, Richard Third, Henry Eighth, Hamlet, and especially Macbeth. I think nothing equals Macbeth." And in January, 1865, Lincoln took time to write a message for an organization commemorating the 106th anniversary of the birth of Robert Burns: "I can not frame a toast to Burns. I can say nothing worthy of his generous heart, and transcendent genius."

Mournful verse appealed to the melancholy strain in Lincoln's nature. His favorite, undoubtedly, was a doleful poem entitled "Mortality." The first two stanzas set the tone:

O why should the spirit of mortal be proud?
Like a swift fleeting meteor—a fast flying cloud
—A flash of the lightning—a break of the wave,
He passeth from life to his rest in the grave.

The leaves of the Oak, and Willow shall fade;
Be scattered around, and together be laid.
And the young and the old, and the low and
  the high,
Shall molder to dust, and together shall lie.

Lincoln himself recounted his first acquaintance with the poem and expressed his regard for it. One of his friends, in the mid-1840s, was a lawyer of Quincy, Illinois, Andrew Johnston, about whom little is known other than that he was an uncle of the Confederate general George E. Pickett, and obtained a West Point appointment for Pickett through Congressman John T. Stuart, Lincoln's first law partner. On February 24, 1846, Lincoln, redeeming a promise, sent Johnston a copy of "Mortality." Johnston acknowledged the receipt of the poem, but Lincoln allowed almost two months to pass before continuing the correspondence. On April 18, from Tremont, Illinois, where he was attending court, he wrote to his friend:

"I have not your letter now before me; but, from memory, I think you ask me who is the author of the piece I sent you, and that you do so ask as to indicate a slight suspicion that I myself am the author. Beyond all question, I am not the author. I would give all I am worth, and go in debt, to be able to write so fine a piece as I think that is. Neither do I know who is the author. I met it in a straggling form in a newspaper last summer, and I remember to have seen it once before, about fifteen years ago, and this is all I know about it."

"Mortality" was, in fact, the work of an obscure Scottish poet, William Knox, who published poems between 1818 and 1825. But to suspect Lincoln of having written it was not unreasonable, for at this time the Springfield lawyer was trying his hand at verse. This he confessed when he sent "Mortality" to Johnston. "By the way," he wrote, "how would you like to see a piece of poetry of my own making? I have a piece that is almost done, but I find a deal of trouble to finish it."

In the same letter in which he denied having written "Mortality" Lincoln wrote:

"The piece of poetry of my own which I alluded to, I was led to write under the following circumstances. In the fall of 1844, thinking I might aid some to carry the State of Indiana for Mr. Clay, I went into the neighborhood in that State in which I was raised, where my mother and only sister were buried, and from which I had been absent about fifteen years. That part of the country is, within itself, as unpoetical as any spot of the earth; but still, seeing it and its objects and inhabitants aroused feelings in me which were certainly poetry; though whether my expression of those feelings is poetry is quite another question. When I got to writing, the change of subjects divided the thing into four little divisions or cantos, the first only of which I send you now and may send the others hereafter.''

On September 6, 1846, Lincoln wrote to Johnston again:

"You remember when I wrote you from Tremont last spring, sending you a little canto of what I called poetry, I promised to bore you with another some time. I now fulfil the promise. The subject of the present one is an insane man. His name is Matthew Gentry. He is three years older than I, and when we were boys we went to school together. He was rather a bright lad, and the son of *the* rich man of our very poor neighbourhood. At the age of nineteen he unaccountably became furiously mad, from which condition he gradually settled down into harmless insanity. When, as I told you in my other letter I visited my old home in the fall of 1844, I found him still lingering in this wretched condition. In my poetizing mood I could not forget the impressions his case made upon me.''

After the text of the Matthew Gentry canto Lincoln closed his letter with the statement: "If I should ever send another, the subject will be a 'Bear hunt.' " He did send Johnston "The Bear Hunt" on February 25, 1847, with a letter which read in part:

"To say the least, I am not at all displeased with your proposal to publish the poetry, or doggerel, or whatever else it may be called, which I sent you. I consent that it may be done, together with the third canto, which I now send you. Whether the prefatory remarks in my letter shall be published with the verses, I leave entirely to your discretion; but let names be suppressed by all means. I have not sufficient hope of the verses attracting any favorable notice to tempt me to risk being ridiculed for having written them."

Johnston published the first two cantos anonymously in the *Quincy Whig* for May 5, 1847, but "The Bear Hunt" never appeared in that paper or anywhere else as far as is known. If Lincoln ever wrote a fourth canto, as he had planned, it has not survived.

Thus ended Lincoln's one serious venture into verse. As a boy he had written a few copybook rhymes, but it is probable that they were folk doggerel (not of his own composition) and for that reason they are not included here. We do include verses he wrote in the autograph books of Rosa and Linnie Haggard, daughters of the proprietor of the Haggard House of Winchester, Illinois, where he stayed for three days during his campaign against Stephen A. Douglas in 1858. We also include a stanza of doggerel, recently discovered, which Lincoln scribbled on the morning of July 19, 1863. The President, according to his secretary, John Hay, was in high good humor: on the first three days of the month Robert E. Lee had been soundly defeated at Gettysburg; on the 14th the Confederate general and his army, badly mauled, had crossed the Potomac on their retreat to Virginia. Lincoln picked up a pen and wrote in a bold hand the four lines with which this book concludes.

Whatever the intrinsic merit of Lincoln's poetry may be—and each reader must make his own appraisal —it is clear that it was not a form of writing at which he would ever excel. Compare his most felicitous lines with the last sentence of the First Inaugural: "The mystic chords of memory, stretching from every battle-field, and patriot grave, to every living heart and hearthstone, all over this broad land, will yet swell the chorus of the Union, when again touched, as surely they will be, by the better angels of our nature." Or with the conclusion of the Gettysburg Address: "It is rather for us to be here dedicated to the great task remaining before us—that from these honored dead we take increased devotion to that cause for which they gave the last full measure of devotion—that we here highly resolve that these dead shall not have died in vain—that this nation, under God, shall have a new birth of freedom —and that government of the people by the people, for the people, shall not perish from the earth." Or finally, the Second Inaugural: "With malice toward none; with charity for all; with firmness in the right, as God gives us to see the right, let us strive on to finish the work we are in; to bind up the nation's wounds; to care for him who shall have borne the battle, and for his widow, and his orphan —to do all which may achieve and cherish a just, and a lasting peace, among ourselves, and with all nations."

Abraham Lincoln had a strong streak of poetry in his nature, but it came out to best advantage in prose.

Paul M. Angle,
Chicago Historical Society

Editorial Note

The first ten stanzas of "My Childhood-home I See Again" exist in two slighly different versions. We present here what appears to be the later one, and hence the one that the author would have preferred. We have set off the second canto and given it the title, "The Maniac," under which it was published in the *Quincy Whig*. The text followed is that of *The Collected Works of Abraham Lincoln* (Rutgers University Press, 1953).

The Collected Poetry of
Abraham Lincoln

My Childhood-home I See Again

My childhood-home I see again,
  And gladden with the view;
And still as mem'ries crowd my brain,
  There's sadness in it too.

O memory! thou mid-way world
  'Twixt Earth and Paradise,
Where things decayed, and loved ones lost
  In dreamy shadows rise.

And freed from all that's gross or vile,
  Seem hallowed, pure, and bright,
Like scenes in some enchanted isle,
  All bathed in liquid light.

As distant mountains please the eye,
  When twilight chases day—
As bugle-tones, that, passing by,
  In distance die away—

As leaving some grand water-fall
  We ling'ring, list it's roar,
So memory will hallow all
  We've known, but know no more.

Now twenty years have passed away,
    Since here I bid farewell
To woods, and fields, and scenes of play
    And school-mates loved so well.

Where many were, how few remain
    Of old familiar things!
But seeing these to mind again
    The lost and absent brings.

The friends I left that parting day—
    How changed, as time has sped!
Young childhood grown, strong manhood grey,
    And half of all are dead.

I hear the lone survivors tell
    How nought from death could save,
Till every sound appears a knell,
    And every spot a grave.

I range the fields with pensive tread,
    And pace the hollow rooms;
And feel (companions of the dead)
    I'm living in the tombs.

The Maniac

A[nd] here's an object more of dread,
    Than ought the grave contains—
A human-form, with reason fled,
    While wretched life remains.

Poor Matthew! Once of genius bright,—
    A fortune-favored child—
Now locked for aye, in mental night,
    A haggard mad-man wild.

Poor Matthew! I have ne'er forgot
    When first with maddened will,
Yourself you maimed, your father fought,
    And mother strove to kill;

And terror spread, and neighbours ran,
    Your dang'rous strength to bind;
And soon a howling crazy man,
    Your limbs were fast confined.

How then you writhed and shrieked aloud,
    Your bones and sinnews bared;
And fiendish on the gaping crowd,
    With burning eye-balls glared.

And begged, and swore, and wept, and prayed,
    With maniac laughter joined—
How fearful are the signs displayed,
    By pangs that kill the mind!

And when at length, tho' drear and long,
    Time soothed your fiercer woes—
How plaintively your mournful song,
    Upon the still night rose.

I've heard it oft, as if I dreamed,
    Far-distant, sweet, and lone;
The funeral dirge it ever seemed
    Of reason dead and gone.

To drink it's strains, I've stole away,
    All silently and still,
Ere yet the rising god of day
    Had streaked the Eastern hill.

Air held his breath; the trees all still
    Seemed sorr'wing angels round.
Their swelling tears in dew-drops fell
    Upon the list'ning ground.

But this is past, and nought remains
    That raised you o'er the brute.
Your mad'ning shrieks and soothing strains
    Are like forever mute.

Now fare thee well: more thou the cause
    Than subject now of woe.
All mental pangs but time's kind laws,
    Hast lost the power to know.

O death! Thou awe-inspiring prince,
    That keepst the world in fear;
Why dost thou tear more blest ones hence,
    And leave him ling'ring here?

    *   *   *   *

And now away to seek some scene
    Less painful than the last—
With less of horror mingled in
    The present and the past.

The very spot where grew the bread
    That formed my bones, I see.
How strange, old field, on thee to tread,
    And feel I'm part of thee!

The editors of *The Collected Works* believe that these last
two stanzas were written as the beginning of a third canto.
If so, Lincoln rejected them as a suitable opening for "The
Bear Hunt."

The Bear Hunt

A wild-bear chace, didst never see?
    Then hast thou lived in vain.
Thy richest bump of glorious glee,
    Lies desert in thy brain.

When first my father settled here,
    'Twas then the frontier line:
The panther's scream, filled night with fear
    And bears preyed on the swine.

But wo for Bruin's short lived fun,
    When rose the squealing cry;
Now man and horse, with dog and gun,
    For vengeance, at him fly.

A sound of danger strikes his ear;
    He gives the breeze a snuff:
Away he bounds, with little fear,
    And seeks the tangled *rough*.

On press his foes, and reach the ground,
    Where's left his half munched meal;
The dogs, in circles, scent around,
    And find his fresh made trail.

With instant cry, away they dash,
        And men as fast pursue;
O'er logs they leap, through water splash,
        And shout the brisk halloo.

Now to elude the eager pack,
        Bear shuns the open ground;
Th[r]ough matted vines, he shapes his track
        And runs it, round and round.

The tall fleet cur, with deep-mouthed voice,
        Now speeds him, as the wind;
While half-grown pup, and short-legged fice,
        Are yelping far behind.

And fresh recruits are dropping in
        To join the merry *corps:*
With yelp and yell,—a mingled din—
        The woods are in a roar.

And round, and round the chace now goes,
        The world's alive with fun;
Nick Carter's horse, his rider throws,
        And more, Hill drops his gun.

Now sorely pressed, bear glances back,
        And lolls his tired tongue;
When as, to force him from his track,
        An ambush on him sprung.

9

Across the glade he sweeps for flight,
    And fully is in view.
The dogs, new-fired, by the sight,
    Their cry, and speed, renew.

The foremost ones, now reach his rear,
    He turns, they dash away;
And circling now, the wrathful bear,
    They have him full at bay.

At top of speed, the horse-men come,
    All screaming in a row.
"Whoop! Take him Tiger. Seize him Drum."
    Bang,—bang—the rifles go.

And furious now, the dogs he tears,
    And crushes in his ire.
Wheels right and left, and upward rears,
    With eyes of burning fire.

But leaden death is at his heart,
    Vain all the strength he plies.
And, spouting blood from every part,
    He reels, and sinks, and dies.

And now a dinsome clamor rose,
    'Bout who should have his skin;
Who first draws blood, each hunter knows,
    This prize must always win.

But who did this, and how to trace
　　What's true from what's a lie,
Like lawyers, in a murder case
　　They stoutly *argufy*.

Aforesaid fice, of blustering mood,
　　Behind, and quite forgot,
Just now emerging from the wood,
　　Arrives upon the spot.

With grinning teeth, and up-turned hair—
　　Brim full of spunk and wrath,
He growls, and seizes on dead bear,
　　And shakes for life and death.

And swells as if his skin would tear,
　　And growls and shakes again;
And swears, as plain as dog can swear,
　　That he has won the skin.

Conceited whelp! we laugh at thee—
　　Nor mind, that not a few
Of pompous, two-legged dogs there be,
　　Conceited quite as you.

To Rosa Haggard

To Rosa—

> You are young, and I am older;
> > You are hopeful, I am not—
> Enjoy life, ere it grow colder—
> > Pluck the roses ere they rot.
>
> Teach your beau to heed the lay—
> > That sunshine soon is lost in shade—
> That *now's* as good as any day—
> > To take thee, Rosa, ere she fade.
> > > A. LINCOLN—

Winchester, Sep. 28. 1858.

To Linnie Haggard

To Linnie—

> A sweet plaintive song did I hear,
> > And I fancied that she was the singer—
> May emotions as pure, as that song set a-stir
> > Be the worst that the future shall bring her.
> > > A. LINCOLN—

Winchester Sep. 30- 1858-

Gen. Lee's Invasion of the North, written by himself—

"In eighteen sixty three, with pomp,
  and mighty swell,
Me and Jeff's Confederacy, went
  forth to sack Phil. del.
The Yankees they got arter us, and
  gin us partic,lar h_ll,
And we skedaddled back again,
  and didn't sack Phil. del."

Written Sunday morning July 19, 1863
Attest John Hay

This book was designed by Michael Stancik
and produced at The Lakeside Press,
R. R. Donnelley & Sons Company,
Chicago, Illinois and Crawfordsville, Indiana.
The typefaces are Arrighi and Centaur.
It is printed on Mohawk Superfine text paper,
and bound in Cockerell marbled paper
with Harper Rotunda end papers.